Greene, Biggs and Graham

Party Edition

by

Prof Politiverse

This is a work of non-fiction.
All of these events described by the Professor actually happened in the
U.S. on Jan 6, 2021 and the days leading up to that fateful day.

First paperback edition October 2022

Book design and illustrations by Prof Politiverse

ISBN 979-8-9871002-3-3 (Hard Cover)
ISBN 979-8-9871002-8-8 (Paperback)
ISBN 979-8-9871002 -6-4 (Kindle)

www.profpolitiverse.com

Note on Fonts: As will be obvious, the Trump-I-Am character speaks in
the Italicized lettering, while the Professor speaks in the Seussian block
lettering. Also, the Professor chose to go with the Georgia font, just to
remind the good readers that it was Georgia that delivered the Senate
to the Democrats. And it is Georgia, specifically Fulton County DA Fani
Willis, holding Donald Trump to account for his attempts to overturn
the election in that fine state.

Note on the timing: The desire was to get this book out before the 2022
midterms, so the Professor wanted to finish the writing of it before the
January 6 Committee hearings resume in September. After he finished
that part, the Search Warrant was executed on Trump's resort in West
Palm Beach, FL. What happens next in the curious case of Defendant
Donald Trump? Stay tuned for the Professor's next book, "One State,
Two States, Red States, Blue States (and Other Fun Stories)."

1

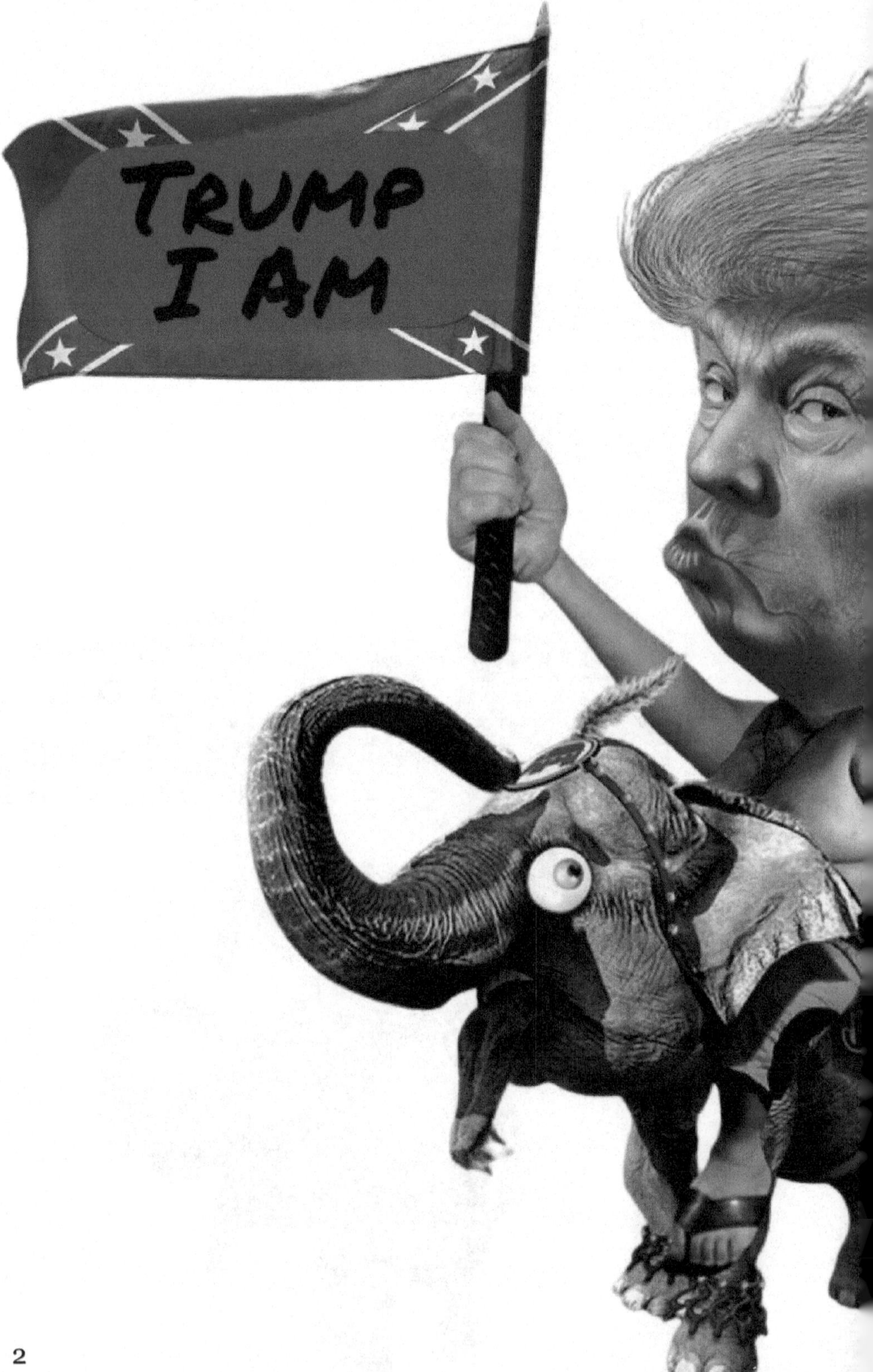
TRUMP
I AM

That Trump-I-Am!
That Trump-I-Am!
I do not like
that MAGA Man!

Do you like Greene, Biggs and Graham?

4

I do not like them, Trump-I-Am.
I do not like Greene, Biggs and Graham!
Andy, Lindsey, and Marjorie Three-Names...
Subverting elections their primary aims.

Would you like them right here or over there?

I would not like them here, there, anywhere,
You can't rescind elections free and fair.
I do not like them in the Deep South,
The closeted one and the rancorous mouth,

Nor that coup-plotter from Arizona...
All three should be shipped to Babylonia!
Insurrectionists should not be admired...
Come November, the R's should all be fired!

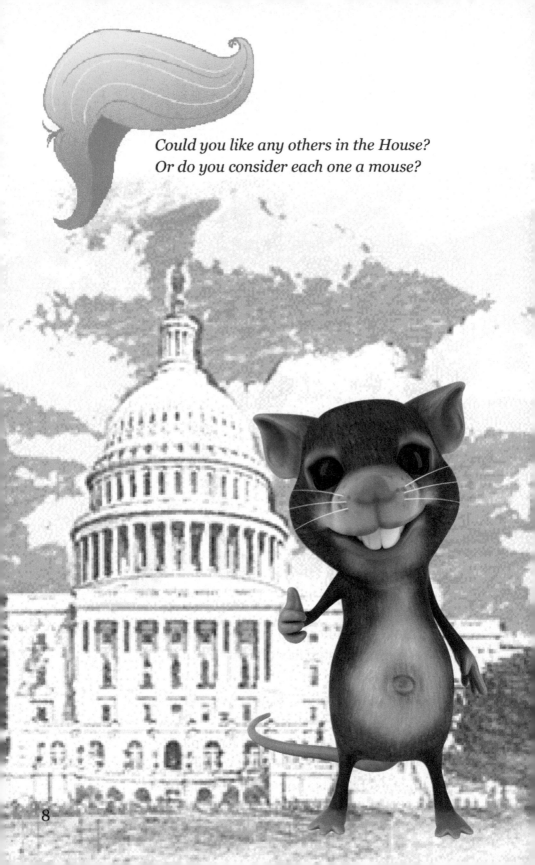

Could you like any others in the House?
Or do you consider each one a mouse?

Well, there's two R's sorta takin' care of biz,
Kinzinger and Cheney...Adam and Liz.
All the rest with their fingers in the wind,
Seeking to avoid the base to offend.

At least these two brave reps want to find out
What happened Jan 6 and hold to account,
Those responsible for inciting a coup...
Mango Madman and his Traitorous Crew.

Do you like the way Laura Ingraham squawks?
Do you believe any of the loons on Fox?

I despise Laura's squawks.
And hell no on the Fox!
I don't want a red house,
Led by Kevin McMouse.

I would not vote for them here or there.
I will never check an R anywhere.
I cannot support Greene, Biggs and Graham
Because you revealed them, Trump-I-Am.

Unleashed the worst versions of themselves,
Within their hearts a dark hatred dwells.
Sometimes I wonder just what I'm seeing,
"Owning the libs" their reason for being.

I won't vote for Greene, Biggs and Graham...
I can't stand them, Trump-I-Am!

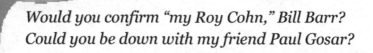

Would you confirm "my Roy Cohn," Bill Barr?
Could you be down with my friend Paul Gosar?

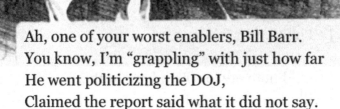

Ah, one of your worst enablers, Bill Barr.
You know, I'm "grappling" with just how far
He went politicizing the DOJ,
Claimed the report said what it did not say.

All along he knew the danger you posed
Every day, that fact is more exposed.
He heaped praise on you on his way out of town,
Knowing well you'd try to burn it all down.

Now on a Reputation Rehabilitation Tour,
Acting as if not part of the Trump Admin Sewer.
Because of charges on Cohen, Lev and Igor,
Barr went after Democrats to even the score.

And coup-coup for Cocoa Puffs, Paul Gosar,
Another crAZy guy gone full fubar!
This guy has had so many epic fails,
His own siblings think he's gone off the rails.

Fancies himself a ninja assassin,
Each act he makes in a racist fashion.
Ali Alexander asked him to play...
He signed up to destroy the US of A!

13

You may like Greene, Biggs and Graham,
You will see,
Look up, you may like them
Up in a tree.

Dammit, get them down from there, if you please...
Like the Lorax, I too speak for the trees.
That your friends are toxic is no surprise,
Like Trump-I-Am, everything they touch dies.

I do not want them all up in the tree,
Not Bill Barr, not Gosar, you let me be.

I do not like all the liars on Fox.
And especially Laura Ingraham's squawks.
I don't want a Republican house,
Collectively, less spine than a mouse.

I won't support them here or there
I like elections free and fair.
I so despise Greene, Biggs and Graham,
Just as I loathe you, Trump-I-Am!

My brain! My brain! My brain! My brain!
You won't believe the size of my brain!
Trump has a very, very large brain!
Could you trust my amazing brain?

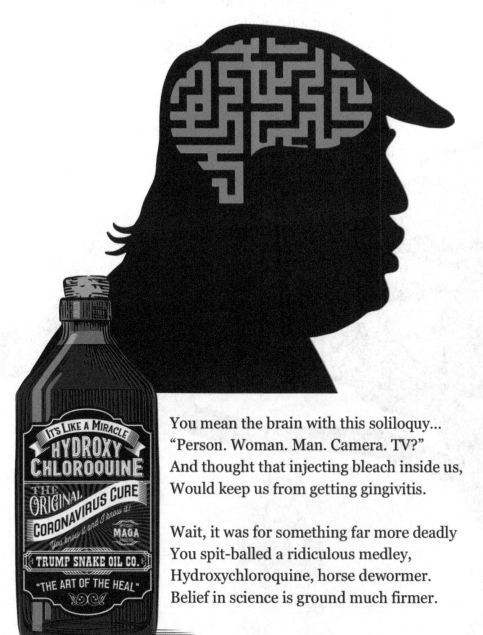

You mean the brain with this soliloquy...
"Person. Woman. Man. Camera. TV?"
And thought that injecting bleach inside us,
Would keep us from getting gingivitis.

Wait, it was for something far more deadly
You spit-balled a ridiculous medley,
Hydroxychloroquine, horse dewormer.
Belief in science is ground much firmer.

So, not with your brain! Not in a tree!
Not with Gosar! Trump, let me be!

It's a hard pass on trusting your brain,
While Merrick cleans up your Bill Barr stain.
Gym Jordan won't speak up for his jocks
Spends all of his time ranting on Fox!

Troth Senchel is your way to tweet now,
An epic failure says Devin's Cow!
The problems aren't only
                    Greene, Biggs and Graham,
The Clown Car overfloweth, Trump-I-Am!

Say, could you support them in the Park?
Come join me on my Lafayette lark.
I'll just have my generals clear our way,
We'll stroll to that church and pretend to pray.

I'll show those protestors who's the boss,
Holding up a Bible under the cross.
I don't care what they're protesting about,
I must show strength, of that there is no doubt.

Cops cleared peaceful folks out with tear gas
For your photo-op so vain and crass.
You held that bible before the crowd,
Two Corinthians would be so proud.

The why of our protest a noble cause,
Fixing our police system's many flaws.
They murdered George Floyd before our eyes,
Yet it's the protesters you demonize.

George's life snuffed out by the murderer Chauvin,
Showing the racism and lies interwoven.
Despite the "sons of bitches" epithets you hurled,
Gianna's daddy did indeed change the world.

Would you bow to me during my reign?
King Donald, master of my domain?

I will not, because you won't get the chance,
In spite of your mouth-breathing sycophants.
America was formed because we don't like kings
Self-rule is the fount from which democracy springs.

Because you broke all the rules and norms
Congress must pass wide-ranging reforms,
To help constrain wannabe dictators
And all of the deplorable traitors.

(And here's one idea Congress should explore,
Don't wait 'til after, it must be done before
One's name on a ballot makes an appearance,
They pass the highest-level security clearance.)

Your cultists believe you were sent by God,
She would've found someone far less flawed.
Paid-off porn stars and a cheated-on wife,
A bankrupt grifter your entire life.

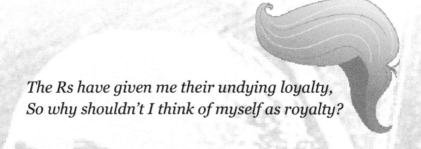

The Rs have given me their undying loyalty,
So why shouldn't I think of myself as royalty?

My name is Inigo Montoya, prepare to cry,
We do not bow down in service to the Big Lie.
You keep using that word "loyalty," it seems,
I do not think it means what you think it means.

You demand loyalty from those who surround you,
Up to and including joining in on your coup.
Yet to you loyalty sure looks like a one-way street,
You would destroy those loyal with merely a tweet.

Thankfully, you're not on Twitter any longer,
Your knockoff site makes it harder to fearmonger.
Funny that Truth Social is actually neither,
A place where truth-telling has taken a breather.

Rudy's cringey appearance on "The Masked Singer,"
Proved the Trump-I-Am stench will always linger.
Rudy's like a boil that continues to fester,
You could make him your Mar-a-Lago court jester!

You will not vote for Greene, Biggs and Graham?

I will not vote for them, Trump-I-Am!

You want us to vote for whom you endorse
Because they're an extension of you, of course.
So, to get a glimpse of your wicked goals,
Let's dig deep into this trio of trolls.

Everybody loves Marj...what's not to like?
She'll be an asset during the Fourth Reich.

Northwest Georgia must be very proud
Of their Marj, so abrasive and loud.
Her followers she continues to fleece...
The rest of us get the gazpacho police.

How could one be so stupid, I wonder.
Another query I sometimes ponder,
As she flails about like a big-eyed fish...
Could she have been hatched in a peachtree dish?

Every conspiracy that comes her way
Gets a new believer that very day.
From Jewish Space Lasers to Stop the Steal,
Her brain powered by a rat on a wheel.

23

Her ignorant tweets sure stick in my craw,
Like, "Trump should just declare 'Marshall Law.'"
Now she says she's a Christian Nationalist,
Proving yet again she ain't no rationalist.
Damn, make it stop; now you're at Bed-minister?
It would be funny if it wasn't so sinister!

After mass shootings, she screams, "Mental Illness!"
Displaying to all her ugly shrillness.
Can't say that that's the problem, then defund it.
"That's in bad faith," opines every pundit.
She's merely an outrage grievance demagogue,
Seeking someone to blame, harassing David Hogg.

Her committee assignments stripped away,
Tried to claim Q-Anon led her astray.
At CPAC, with a Jan 6 Defendant she prayed,
They're political martyrs she tries to persuade.
But doesn't she also claim it was antifa?
Sure sounds like a case of selective amnesia!

Even though she's one of the right's rising stars,
She should get used to being behind those bars.
Wanted a pardon for her role in the plot,
She must've known she was going to get caught.
One only needs a pardon when they've done a crime,
Marj can do her CrossFit pullups while serving time.

How could you not support my friend Andy?
He makes insurrections go down like candy.

As he sits behind his 5th District desk,
Andy's beliefs have always been grotesque.
Wants no exceptions for rape or incest,
Subjugating women his lifelong quest.

With anti-Semites, he headlined a luncheon,
Then tried to prevent government function...
Voted no on passing covid relief,
Sharing with gay folks against his beliefs.

This guy's got many hairbrained ideas,
Like ranting on the size of tortillas.
Says about that, they don't want you talking...
Ignored his subpoena, just kept walking.

Biggs at the time was the "Freedom Caucus Chair,"
While he subverted elections free and fair.
These Freedom Caucus folks, from where I sit,
Seem like flies, attracted to your bullshit.

Mark Meadows once sat in the chairman's seat,
Before calling in to the "War Room" suite.
Other Caucus folks like Jordan and Perry,
Of course, tried to help you with your Hail Mary.

Biggs planned and schemed with Paul, Mo and Ali
To set up and invite folks to a rally.
Not just any rally, but one to "Stop the Steal."
They'd do all this for you? I don't get the appeal.

Andy worked hard on the Electors Fraud,
And his call to Rusty seemed rather odd.
Sought a pardon for his part in the scheme...
Cheating seems to be the Republican theme.

The one good thing we can say of Lindsey,
He's not the ass waging war on Disney.
We'll get to that doughy one in a bit,
For now, reflect on what Graham did admit...

As part of Lindsey's stinging rebuke,
Called Trump-I-Am a jackass and a kook...
Four years of chaos left me a bit hazy,
But didn't he call you unfit and crazy?

Didn't hold back, his mouth like a spigot,
"Trump's a race-baiting xenophobic bigot!"
Back in '16, when it came time to choose,
He chose over you one Rafael Cruz.

"Trump's the most flawed nominee in history,"
Over golf, something changed...'tis a mystery.
Could you be holding Russian kompromat
Over this piece of Republican rot?

I don't agree with Lindsey Graham on much,
But he can charm with his southerner's touch.
He didn't vote against certification,
And seemed appalled by your insurrection.

He shouldn't be in this poetry slam...
But I needed a name that sounds like "ham."
And the act that certainly sealed his fate,
The call to Georgia's Secretary of State.

Okay, that thing I just said, I was just wrong,
For his threats, Lindsey absolutely does belong.
"If Trump's indicted, there will be riots in the streets."
I'm fairly certain the DOJ's bringin' receipts.

In the past, he rolled with a decent man...
Now Lindsey seems to be your biggest fan.
"I'm out" he said, before jumping back in,
Being Trump's wingman his original sin.

Lindsey once said, "Use my words against me,"
So, when he came to you on bended knee
He proved what we've always known to be true,
He's but a steaming pile of number two.

What about the "leaders" who played along?
They let me keep singing my "stop the steal" song.

Your enablers were from many levels,
It's in the details we'll find the devils.
First, soft supporters who just wouldn't say
That Biden won 'til that December day.

"What's the harm humoring him for a while?
He'll send out some tweets with 'stop the steal' bile,
Then Joe Biden will be our new president."
But you kept lying, not remotely hesitant.

Rob, Marco, Mike and Mitch fall into this camp,
In fact, Mitch is the current double-speak champ.
On one hand, he says you are guilty as sin,
Then cowardly leaves action up to the Dems.

Another group that belongs on this tier
Those who to the law took pains to adhere.
But then made sure that we knew where they stood,
They'd again vote for you, but of course they would.

Rusty Bowers, to his eternal shame,
And that guy from Georgia with the weird-ass name,
Both said sure, they would vote for Trump again,
And toss our country into the rubbish bin.

It's hard to finish a book with crimes ongoing,
And all the stupidity never slowing.
But Rusty surprised us and went the other way,
"I'll never vote for Trump," he finally did say.

What about states making it harder to vote?
I'll soon have this democracy by the throat.

This layer worse than the "humor him" crowd,
They're just saying the quiet part out loud.
And what could be their excuse du jour?
"Folks must believe their elections secure."

But they were secure, and that's known to all,
Your minions though played along in thrall.
You lied so much about voter fraud,
Everyone knew it merely a façade.
A way for you to come to terms with your loss,
But states soon saw it as their secret sauce.

Florida and Georgia have been two of the worst,
With Governors DeSantis and Kemp they've been cursed.

Florida's guy, the doughy one mentioned before,
On Disney and gay folks declared all-out war.
Now he's demanding students declare a side,
This intimidation we cannot abide.

Georgia, the heart of the political world,
In the most racist way, their new law unfurled.
Close polling places to create lengthy waits,
Then make it a crime to help their thirst abate.

One of the most amazing orators I've ever heard,
The Senator who moonlights spreading the word.
We'll leave this theme with the good pastor's quote...
"Some people don't want some people to vote."

What about all the reps who are on my side?
And senators aiding the democracy slide?

The next tier are the Repugs who voted,
'Cause to Donald Trump they're so devoted,
To overturn the will of the voters,
And satisfy all of you "fraud" promoters.

I'm not a fan of right-wing philosophy,
But my objections here aren't on policy.
Anyone who voted to overturn
Is someone the voters should surely spurn.

This group a hundred-forty-seven strong
Let's talk about two from this fact-free throng.

"I like Ted Cruz more than my colleagues like Ted Cruz."
Al Franken jokes, "And I really hate Ted Cruz!"
A cheap rhyme I know, but never fails to amuse,
Ted's "Green Eggs and Ham" reading a misuse of Seuss.

When the guv's policies caused Texans to die,
That, Ted Cruz thought, the time to take to the sky.
His Cancun trip a contemptible decision,
Treats his constituents with deep derision.

And who can give Ted a run for his money?
Josh Hawley, who made running so damn funny.
In support of rioters, he wasn't shy.
But the will of the voters, he'll just run by.

I thought the raised fist was his Greg Stillson shot,
Nope, 'twas the running so he wouldn't get caught!
This tough-guy "manhood" schtick is but a crock,
Josh Hawley, a national laughingstock!

One more thing before we take this to press,
Senate R's keep putting our vets in distress.
Voted no as if burn pit cancers aren't real,
Ted's fist bump showcases their cruelty and zeal.

BREAKING NEWS
AZ GOP STATE REP. DODGES QUESTIONS ABOUT HIS INVOLVEMENT IN FAKE-ELECTOR SCHEME

Aaron Rupar ✪
@atrupar Follow

apparently fake Michigan electors who said they were
working with the Trump campaign planned to hide out in
the Michigan Capitol overnight

#WARD4US

Won't you support my fake electors scheme,
And help me fulfill my autocratic dream?

The next worst group of folks we'll never support,
The state electors who attempted to thwart
The will of the voters who had made their choice,
An illegal effort to drown out our voice!

A conspiracy led by the Trump-I-Am team,
An unlawful agreement so it would seem.
Seven states, six battlegrounds plus one more,
Eighty-four electors a solemn oath swore.

A point-person chosen for each of the states,
Trump-I-Am desperate, facing dire straits,
Pressured these people to fraudulently swear,
That they were duly elected, they did declare.
Then sent their fraud documents through the mail,
That's wire fraud, each charge twenty years in jail.

Pennsylvania's point was a man named Doug,
The lust for power a dangerous drug.
Mastriano, the R's nominee for Guv,
A Nationalist seeking guidance from "above."

Burt Jones signed on as a Georgia elector,
Now he's running for Lieutenant Governor.
This is one guy who should the door be shown,
They don't get to put Trump-I-Am on a throne.

That Arizona lawyer's emails with Boris,
These eighty-four part of a lawbreaking chorus.
"That's so funny, Ari," let's a different path take,
"Alternate electors" might be better than "fake."

CERTIFICATE OF THE VOTES OF THE
2020 ELECTORS FROM GEORGIA

LG candidate's involvement in 'fake' electors draws scrutiny

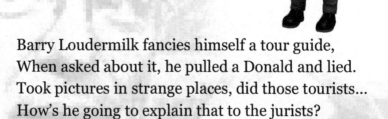

You gotta love my congressional R's, right?
Look how much they aided my "stop the steal" sleight!

The tightening ring who helped in your plots,
Known collectively as the traitor tots...
The usual suspects, obnoxious and raucous,
The Congressional Co-Conspirator Caucus.

This election mafia group numbers twenty,
Of Gosar, Cruz, Greene, Biggs & Graham,
                                I've said plenty.
Let's get a refresher on the rest of the gang
That wanted democracy to go out with a bang.

Barry Loudermilk fancies himself a tour guide,
When asked about it, he pulled a Donald and lied.
Took pictures in strange places, did those tourists...
How's he going to explain that to the jurists?

Mike Lee connected you with a lawyer quite shady,
She's infamously now known as the Kraken Lady.
"She has a strategy to keep things alive,"
A cockamamie plan she did surely contrive.

Mike Pence nearly received from bagman Ron Johnson,
Fraudulent slates from Michigan and Wisconsin.
Ron said he didn't feel threatened on Jan 6,
Then trotted out the usual racist tricks.

Madison Cawthorne helped organize the rally,
Then beat up a tree in the middle of a valley.
One could rightly say his career hit a speed bump,
When he spoke of your side's orgies and key-bumps.

We've been down this Georgia road more than twice,
Barry and Marjorie and now Jody Hice.
He tweeted "it's our 1776 moment,"
Then fought for a King Donald enthronement.

Texas coming in strong with Brian Babin,
All of these folks okay with your pussy-grabbin'!
Yet another at the 12/21 meeting,
Planning out how they'll sell all the cheating.

At that December meeting was Andy Harris,
Come on Maryland, aren't you a little embarrassed?
Now their Republicans nominated Dan Cox,
Can't you see that they want to turn back the clocks?

Ronny Jackson kept safe by a militia group,
Landing him in a big pot of Oath Keeper soup.
The doctor who claimed you weighed 239,
'Cause obesity, you couldn't be over the line.

Matt Gaetz was at the meeting, but hold the phone,
Pardons from "the boss" discussed with Roger Stone.
Blanket pardon sought from the beginning of time,
To keep him from paying for sex trafficking crimes.

Lauren Boebert, even before taking her seat,
Helped plan ways to ensure the overturn complete.
Rumors swirl of tours led by this malcontent,
Tweeted telling the attackers where Nancy went.

In Civics, Mo Brooks must've been skipping class,
We don't choose by "taking down names and kicking ass."
He helped arrange the December 21 meeting,
And proved their devotion to democracy fleeting.

One of the ringleaders was Louie Gohmert,
To change the results took actions quite overt.
To compel he interfere, Louie sued Mike Pence,
Then sought a pardon, for his crimes have no defense.

Jim Jordan helped with your strategy sessions,
Phone calls with you among his many confessions.
He called your chief of staff during the attack,
Asked about pardons after the capital sacked.

Scott Perry is apparently a real rapscallion,
Pushed a theory about satellites Italian,
Wanted Jeffrey Clark installed over at Justice,
To the states send a letter,
                              "There's fraud, just trust us."

Kevin McCarthy is your most loyal lapdog,
Revived your career on that Mar-a-Lago slog.
Claimed you accepted some responsibility,
Quite dubious given you lack that ability.
Beliefs tossed aside for the one thing he seeks,
For the "Speaker" role, this guy is much too weak!

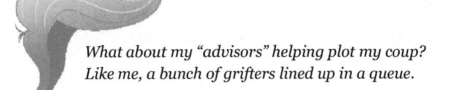

What about my "advisors" helping plot my coup?
Like me, a bunch of grifters lined up in a queue.

Somehow along the way, you've managed to collect,
A group wanting to see the body politic wrecked.
Or as Frumpy Two-Shirts says in a voice that grates,
"Deconstruction of the administrative state."

This collection of weirdness leaves one aghast,
Each one more comically evil than the last.
Reflecting on their damage leaves me deliriou
It would be funny if it wasn't so serious.

You've always liked to collect shiny pieces,
And all the havoc they wreak never ceases.
I like to call them the "Inner Circle from Hell,"
Let's take a tour down into the gutters they dwell.

I've never liked when the press mashes up names,
But "Javanka" is so bad it went down in flames.
Ivanka cashed in on her role in the White House,
Jared and the money, a fox in the henhouse.
Of your nepotism, these two took full advantage,
From the Saudis, Jared got $2Bil to manage.

An obscure legal theory got in your ear,
John Eastman told you what you wanted to hear.
He said the Vice President we must convince,
The power he holds in his hands is immense.
If he delays the Vote Certification,
You can keep up with your autocrat flirtation.

An environmental lawyer named Jeffrey Clark,
Attempted to make a dirty deal with a shark.
Make him Attorney General and he'll grant your wish,
He'll say that there was fraud unlike that other squish.
You made him acting AG for just a day,
But with "Go wait for an oil spill," he was brushed away.

These next two are into the home goods they sell,
Their names are Patrick Byrne and Mike Lindell.
One fancies himself a pillow artisan,
I prefer my bedding to be nonpartisan.
The other for a White House meeting just stopped by,
We all know him better as the Overstock Guy.
Can someone please explain what the hell they were doing,
Sticking their noses in an electorate screwing?

This crazy woman claimed it was Hugo Chavez,
That even though dead somehow changed votes for Prez.
Sidney Powell, the shady lawyer mentioned before,
Said things no reasonable person would fall for.
She said just that in a defamation case,
But in public, wild conspiracies embraced.
Voting machines and Venezuelan hackin,'
All somehow part of "Releasing the Kraken."

What the hell happened to "America's mayor?"
Back in the day a prosecution conveyor.
Rudy was so desperate to remain relevant,
He became a free agent for Team Malevolent.
Rudy Giuliani, with his hands in his pants,
A fraud case with no evidence tried to advance.
At a presser, to show just how low they were scraping,
He spoke at the famed Four Seasons Total Landscaping.
His face melting like in that great scene from "Raiders,"
Shouted "Trial by Combat" to a field full of traitors.

Peter Navarro is one who took a hard right,
He was arrested just before boarding a flight.
He ignored his subpoena and stomped his feet,
Thought in an election it's okay to cheat.
In this "Stop the Steal" con, this guy is knee-deep,
He's still pushing his dubious Green Bay Sweep.

This powerhouse couple is quite an aberrance,
We know them as Ginni and her husband Clarence.
Her texts and emails part of an insurrection,
On providing proof, he was the only objection.
Clarence and his wife are two peas in a pod,
On this country inflicted thirty years of fraud.
Ginni wants to send democracy down the tubes,
He's still angry over high-tech coke cans and pubes.

Mark Meadows just sitting on a couch doom-scrolling,
While his reckless boss he should've been controlling.
Rumors you're going to throw him under the bus,
Mark should've known you are one that no one can trust.
Meadows' phone the waystation for texts of all kind,
"Someone is going to get killed," need we remind.
"He thinks that Pence deserves it," Mark told Cipollone,
Things got "real, real bad" while you pushed more baloney.

The question of who ruined politics is moot,
But it can surely be traced back to a man named Newt.
Opponents can't just have different points of view,
"They're demons and baby-killers," his toxic stew.
The Clinton Impeachment led by Mr Gingrich,
While cheating on his wife, the irony is rich.
Now they're telling us he was involved with Jan 6,
Reached into his usual bag of dirty tricks.

One of the worst is Mike Flynn, generally speaking,
Flirtations with Q, and all his attention-seeking.
Grievance at being fired became his fixation,
Led chants of "Lock Her Up" at your coronation.
Your Security Advisor for a short time,
Lying to the feds about the Russians his crime.
Of course you pardoned him on your way out the door,
Now he headlines the ReAwaken carnival tour.
He's got wild theories on the covid vaccines,
Urged the military to seize voting machines.
His looniness exposed during his deposition,
Pled the fifth when asked about peaceful transition.

HERE COMES THE FOUR WORST...

Stephen Miller, in your White House one of the brashest,
Known better as "C+ Santa Monica fascist."
You made him your Czar on all things Immigration,
And now we all know he's not an aberration.
He was the point person on your cruel Muslim ban,
And author of your family separation plan.
"The President's powers here are beyond question,"
The poster child of Trump-I-Am's cruel aggression.

Alex Jones, one of the most evil men on earth,
Selling his banality has increased his net worth.
What he has done to the Sandy Hook parents,
Something we should all call out in abhorrence.
His constant lies made their lives a living hell,
But makes big money on the prepper gear he sells.
His call to "show our numbers" after your "Be Wild" tweet,
Showed us your plan without being remotely discreet.
Hope that all he's made from the lies he embraces,
Gets taken from him in the defamation cases.

Steve Bannon, the Frumpy Two-Shirts mentioned before,
A chaos agent in this political war.
On a mission to torch the R's establishment wing,
Out of his podcast fans, every dollar he'll wring.
"I haven't begun to fight" he told the reporters,
But "We Build the Wall" was bilking your supporters.
You didn't care because your whole thing is the grift,
His pardon on your last day a nice parting gift.
He plans to put MAGA in at the local level,
To destroy democracy for which he will revel.
Bannon was the point over at the Willard War Room,
Tried to kill Biden's presidency deep in the womb.

I saved Roger Stone until the end of the line,
He's been a 'dirty trickster' for a long damn time.
A purveyor of darkness for many a year,
With that top hat, round glasses, and villainous sneer.
He was around when Tricky Dick fell from grace,
And had his hand in the Brooks Brothers riot case.
Let's not forget he was the contact for Guccifer,
And helped Russia install President Lucifer.
To top off his illustrious evil career,
Helped you on Jan 6 as the chief mutineer.
You pardoned him for what he did up to that point,
May all his treasonous acts land him in the joint.

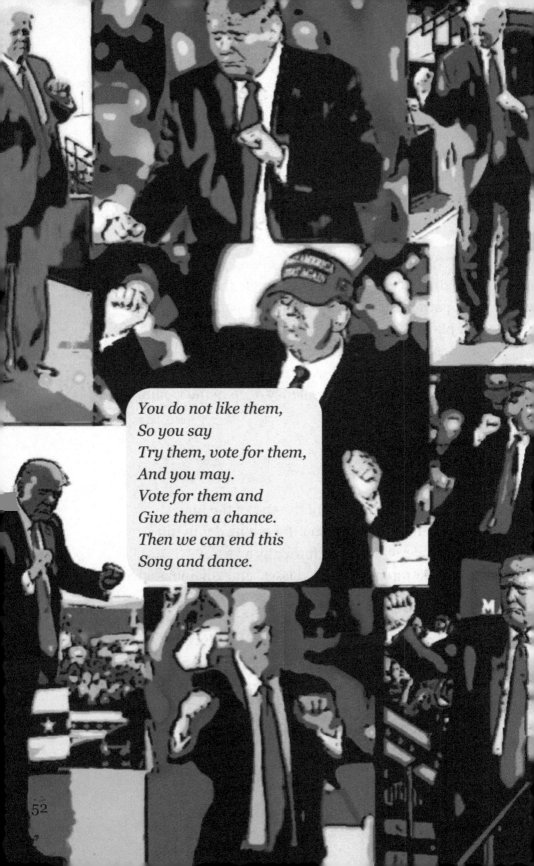

Trump-I-Am, you could never persuade me
To go and vote for this ridiculous three,
Or any of your ragtag crackpot gang
Who would've been fine to see Mike Pence hang.

But you clearly convinced millions of folks to cast,
A vote to take us back to some idyllic past.
You got enough votes in just the right places,
Conspired with Russia to cover your bases.

I feel like folks need to be reminded,
Even those who by Fox have been blinded.
Let's take a long look back at this "idyllic" state,
And determine if you made America great.

Say! I was right all along about you,
This American Carnage you spoke of came true!
As we closed out the Trump-I-Am administration,
It felt like you had set fire to our once-great nation.
And here we are, two years since you got booted out,
We're sitting on a powder keg, while you still pout.

On that November day back in 2016,
I thought, we're heading into something obscene.
But as bad as I knew you were going to be,
That pales in comparison to what we all had to see.
Never has a president been so cruel and lawless,
It's been a firehose of chaos that you brought us.
Let's take a rocky trip down memory lane,
To see how you treated this country with disdain.

You invited and won with help from the Russians,
Never considered the vast repercussions.
Then you with your tail dragging in Helsinki,
"I don't see any reason why it would be."
Justice obstructed and pardons dangled,
The Mueller Report Barr certainly mangled.

Then you showed who you are in the Charlottesville wreck.
Did you show any decency? Nope, not a speck!
Phrases chanted like "Jews will not replace us,"
And "Blood and Soil," so vile and racist.
You couldn't disparage them; this was your base.
"Good people on both sides" just wasn't the case!
A young lady run down, her name Heather Heyer,
By the Confederates and Nazis you so admire.

A monster who would throw children in cages,
Your cruel depravity still enrages!
The "family values" party is who supports you,
Splitting up these families is what you resort to.
There's no "family values" in this vicious action,
That they were immigrants merely a distraction.
When someone shows you who they are, believe them,
You're an evil man spreading hatred and mayhem.

Mueller testified, and the following day,
You thought, "they aren't able to make me pay."
So you jumped on the phone and did some extortion,
Throwing out your "perfect phone call" distortion.
You held up our defensive aid to Ukraine,
Unless dirt on Biden they would help you obtain.
Now your friend Putin is on a killing spree,
After your shakedown of President Zelenskyy.
Adam Schiff warned us that you'd do it again,
Ladies and gentlemen, your moment of Zen.

In the early days of the election year,
News of a health scare we began to hear.
This covid thing was spreading like wildfire,
Soon bodies were thrown upon the funeral pyre.

News of epidemic prevention funding you cut,
Hit the news and the web like a punch to the gut.
Studies on emerging infectious diseases
And outbreak detection you put funding freezes.

Since it began in California and New York,
You decided the Blue States should do all the work.
You made the states fight over the resources,
Instead of working together and joining forces.

To Woodward in Feb, you said it was deadly,
"It's airborne Bob," and infects us more readily.
In his "Rage" book, he wrote that you stated,
You always deliberately downplayed it.
While telling us in ways most satirical,
"One day it will disappear like a miracle."

The pandemic raged and the nation trembled,
To fight it, a Special Task Force assembled.
A comprehensive plan to test for infection,
Scrapped 'cause it wouldn't help your reelection.
The team, led by Jared Kushner, helped you decide,
You'd just let this be a Blue State Genocide.

At the presser, you looked over at Dr Birx,
Throwing shit against the wall to see what works.
Nothing ever did, so you kept on lying,
"Fauci's against me," you wouldn't stop crying.

Your need to minimize covid led to this gem,
"I made the vaccines, but you shouldn't trust them."
Your team had no plans to get shots in arms,
Your anti-vax drive caused horrific harms.

As Americans were dying, and the world watched,
It became clear that our response had been botched.
A Democratic hoax your ridiculous claim,
Obama, Biden and China were all to blame.

Your malignant narcissism led the way,
To three thousand covid deaths every day.
You fought the science, and we rolled the dice,
A million-plus lives lost a terrible price!

The Trump-I-Am crowning achievement,
Your most brazen act of deceivement...
"Frankly, we did win this election," you said,
Before the votes counted and folks went to bed.

From that point forward, you shouted the Big Lie,
On your propaganda machine, you could rely.
Funny that "fraud" is always in urban areas,
Feeding the right-wing bubble hysteria.

About your Big Lie, there's something I've wondered,
If there was fraud, wasn't it you who blundered?
In '16, you claimed fraud stole the popular vote,
"I alone can fix it," your most bombastic quote.

Chris Krebs and CISA made our elections secure,
No Russians to help you this time, they did ensure.
The irony that this is the one thing you fixed...
Sticking with your pattern, Krebs promptly was nixed.

The fact remains that there was never any fraud,
You lost 'cause your presidency was oh so flawed.
You saw the polls and knew you were going to lose,
"If I don't win, it's rigged," you began to accuse.

You know that that's not how democracies work,
Beneath that orange skin, an autocrat lurks.
You look over at Hungary, jealous of Orbán,
Decided it was time to run Trump's Greatest Con.

You activated the Proud Boys during the debate,
"Stand back and stand by," you said, sealing their fate.
The Three Percenters also awaited your call,
The Oath Keepers sought to help the Capitol fall.

You summoned them to come for a big protest,
"Will be wild," you tweeted, turns out not in jest.
They weren't the only ones to answer your call,
Turns out thousands wanted to join your cabal.

You assembled them to rally at the Ellipse,
Some hung out in trees with assault rifle clips.
"They're not here to hurt me," you said with a grin,
"Get those mags out of here, let my people in."

You lit the flame of the capitol attack,
Soldiers soon climbing in the formation stack.
You fanned the flames with your infamous tweet,
On the VP, your ground troops turned up the heat.

You gleefully watched the unfolding violence,
One hundred eighty-seven minutes of silence.
Finally, you told those attacking the police,
"We love you, you're special, go home, go in peace."

You are responsible for all the death that day,
And the injuries and trauma, for which you will pay.
But for the damage you've caused this nation once great,
Dante's Deepest Circle of Hell surely your fate.

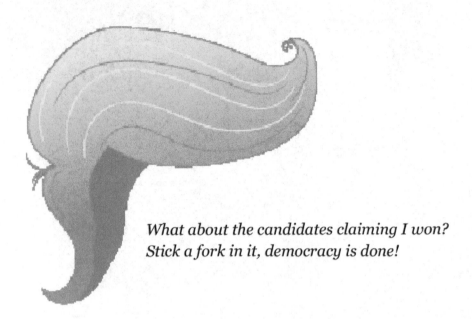

What about the candidates claiming I won?
Stick a fork in it, democracy is done!

The party formerly thought of as conservative,
Has gone to a place where facts are alternative.
They nominate people with but one desire,
Their platform has one plank: Election Denier.

You've endorsed so many across the nation,
I guess you've got some cause for celebration.
Quite a few in your camp their primaries have won,
But come November, we'll see just who's having fun.

In Pennsylvania, it's like you are Santa Claus,
Endorsing a quack from New Jersey, "Doctor" Oz.
In Georgia, you backed a football star named Walker,
Brain damage shows he could've used better blockers.

You have set your Arizona party on fire,
Can't win a primary if not a denier.
You endorsed Gosar, Lake, Masters and Finchem,
Folks tired of your shit will come out to bench 'em.

You think that all anyone should care about,
Your election loss, which was frankly a blowout.
And that seems to be what your party latched onto,
I don't understand this victimhood they're drawn to.

The election was never stolen from you,
With your chaos and drama, voters were through.
You deniers can keep crying about the past,
While the Dems keep working getting good stuff passed.

So, I won't vote for Greene, Biggs & Graham,
I'll never vote for them, Trump-I-Am,
I won't support those from the "Humor Him" crowd,
Humoring Trump-I-Am is never allowed.

I won't back any R who helped pass a new law,
Well, I wouldn't anyway, but that's the last straw.
Any in Congress against certification,
My dollars will go towards their termination.

I'll knock doors against any involved in the scheme,
The fake electors in jail a prosecutor's dream.
Those twenty we all know as the Traitor Tots,
When they go down, I got the next round of shots.

I'll be kickin' back with a big popcorn bowl,
While your inner circle pleads for parole.
And for nominating those who can't say you lost,
The Republican party is going to pay a huge cost.

Can't you see your way to voting for me?
Trump-I-Am gets the best ratings, don't you see?

When the history is written of this time,
It will make no sense, no reason or rhyme.
How did this party base so agrarian,
Fall in love with this gaudy vulgarian?

In the small town where I spent my growing-up years,
I don't remember folks always preying on fears.
Integrity and respect got pushed to the side,
In favor of bullying, threats, anger and pride.

Those in the heartland feel that they're looked down upon,
Hating those different is the conclusion they've drawn.
You've amplified that with cruelty of all kind,
Folks, electing Trump didn't change anyone's mind.

They showed who they are by electing this racist,
This obnoxious joke whose instincts are the basest.
They love Trump because he wants to hurt those they hate,
So being looked down on is naturally their fate.

Rusty Bowers said something that bears repeating,
"I do not want to be a winner by cheating."
But to the R's, cheating now seems to be okay,
If they get what they want at the end of the day.
And what they seem to want is more Trump-I-Am,
A cheater extraordinaire just ain't my jam!

As we approach this epic poem's final stanza,
I must say you remind me of George Costanza.
If you worked as hard at your job as you did on a coup,
You might've won, keeping at bay your traitorous crew.

But you chose to gaslight us on this deadly disease,
Your ineptitude brought this country to its knees.
You didn't know how to govern or care to learn,
It was always the adulation for which you yearn.
Your supporters too proud to admit they were wrong,
A life of public service is not where you belong.

I'm of two minds on whether you run again,
What if a seismic event were to help you to win?
Your Republican base seems to be excited,
To nominate you again even if indicted.
Your feeble brain believes that you're safe if you run,
Kicking your ass a third time will be endless fun.

But the answer to your question is not just no,
It's "Hell no," and for you methinks it's time to go!
Begone with you, you loser political hack,
The fifties just called; they want their racism back!
And could you do us a solid as we bid you adieu?
Take this ridiculous thing called Trumpism with you!

Thank you, kind readers, for joining me for a spell,
As we bid the Orange Jesus a not-so-fond farewell.
Even though I asked him to please take it with,
Trumpism leaving with him would be merely a myth.

His addiction to Big Macs could take him tomorrow,
The mini-Trumps in his wake his playbook would borrow.
"Trump without the baggage" makes them seem more appealing,
But their autocratic bent they're constantly revealing.

It seems appropriate with this last set of rhymes,
That we've ripped Trump in verse 420 times.
Republican stunts show they're high on their own supply,
When Trump's gone, we'll soon have Florida fish to fry.

Acknowledgements

I want to thank my amazing wife, who indulged me in this passion project... I love you!

And thanks go out to the great Dr Seuss, Shel Silverstein and others who brought this love of all things whimsical.

Attribution to DonkeyHokey for several of his fabulous caricature renderings of the loathsome Trumpkins. All are slightly modified...

- Pg 1-2: "Donald Trump's Southern Strategy" is licensed under CC BY-SA 2.0. Removed background and added Sharpie writing on the confederate flag.
- Pg 4: "Marjorie Taylor Greene - Caricature" and "Lindsey Graham - Caricature," both licensed under CC BY 2.0. Mashed up with an Andy Biggs illustration and put through a PencilSketch app to create the titular "Greene, Biggs and Graham" Mashup.
- Pg 17: "2016 Republican Clown Car Parade -Trump Exta Special Edition" is licensed under CC BY-SA 2.0. Added Devin's Cow to the mix and put it through a PencilSketch app.
- Pg 52-53: "Donald Trump - Riding the Wrecking Ball" is licensed under CC BY-SA 2.0. Modified to be part of the American Carnage Mashup then put through the PencilSketch app.

https://creativecommons.org/licenses/by/2.0/

Pg 7: On the Arizona-Babylonia rhyme, of course attribution goes to the great Steve Martin and his satirical song "King Tut," from 1978.

Pg 14: Reference to "The Lorax," another one of Dr Seuss's great books.

Pg 14: Reference to a book by Lincoln Project co-founder Rick Wilson, "Everything Trump Touches Dies."

Pg 21: Reference to the great character Inigo Montoya from the classic movie, "The Princess Pride," played by Mandy Patinkin.

Pg 23: Reference to the Dave Matthews Band song, "Big-Eyed Fish" – Sorry it's about Marj, Dave, just needed a rhyme for peachtree dish.

Pg 35: In an Aug 1, 2022 interview with John Karl, Rusty Bowers said that he would not vote for Trump again after previously saying that he would.

Pg 37: Attribution to Sen Raphael Warnock, on his work and quote, "Some people don't want some people to vote."

Pg 38: Attribution to Al Franken and his great joke about Ted Cruz.

Pg 38: Another reference to a Dr Seuss book, "Green Eggs & Ham," because Ted Cruz read it on the Senate floor.

Pg 40: Reference for the list of Fake Electors:
https://www.newsfromthestates.com/article/trumps-fake-electors-heres-full-list

Pg 40: Attribution to MSNBC for the screen grab of AZ State Rep Jake Hoffman, dodging questions about his involvement in the Fraudulent Electors Scheme.

Pg 40: Attribution to Aaron Rupar on his tweet on the Fraudulent Electors from the State of Michigan planning to hide out overnight in the Michigan State Capitol.

Pg 40: Attribution to the Republican Party of AZ for their confessional tweet of their involvement in the Fraudulent Electors Scheme.

Pg 40: Attribution to the Atlanta Journal Constitution for the headline on the Republican candidate for Lt. Governor being one of the 16 Fraudulent Electors from GA.

Pg 41: Attribution to Ari Melber's MSNBC show "The Beat" for the Jan 21, 2022 episode where he interviewed Boris Epshteyn, "That's so funny, Ari."

Pg 43: Attribution to the line from Sheryl Crow's song "Every Day is a Winding Road," '...been down this road more than twice.'

Pg 50: Attribution to Jon Lovett and the rest of the Pod Save America crew, on their very apt moniker for Stephen Miller, "C+ Santa Monica fascist."

Pg 51: While not intended, the verse about Roger Stone definitely has a "Sympathy for the Devil" vibe, so I should give attribution to the apparently eternal Rolling Stones.

Pg 58: Attribution to the great Maya Angelou and her quote, "When people show you who they are, believe them."

Pg 59: Attribution to the inimitable Jon Stewart, his closing line from his time on "The Daily Show," 'Ladies and gentlemen, your moment of Zen.' Many thanks go to Jon for the work he does for our veterans and first responders.

Pg 61: Reference to the "Prevail" podcast by Greg Olear, the Blue State Genocide episode in particular.

Pg 61: Quotation marks around a Trump-I-Am statement, "I made the vaccines, but you shouldn't trust them." It is not a direct quote...it was an effort to show the dichotomy between his claiming credit for the vaccines while at the same time through words and action/inaction, saying that we the public shouldn't trust them.

Pg 62: A tiny mistruth...I wrote that "I alone can fix it" was Trump-I-Am's most bombastic quote when it is really his 2nd most bombastic quote. From the home office in the heart of Trump Country, the #1 most bombastic quote by Trump-I-Am... " I am the chosen one." https://youtu.be/_JsAQj36gCU

Pg 67: "Kicking your ass a third time..." is of course meant in the popular vote sense. If you run, the next time it is going to be somewhere in the range of 10-15 million votes. Enjoy the remainder of your days dealing with your legal issues, Donald...all because you got big mad when Barack Obama mercilessly mocked you!

Pg 75: Reference to George Costanza from 'Seinfeld' fame, who worked harder at staying unemployed than he ever did when actually working.

Pg 78: An acknowledgement on one of the acknowledgements, the one from page 62. Of course, "From the home office in..." is a schtick from one of the greats in his long-running show, "Late Night with David Letterman."

Coming soon:
One State, Two States, Red States, Blue States (and Other Fun Stories)

Made in the USA
Columbia, SC
23 December 2022

72726240R00046